DEREK

A YANKEE FOR THE NEW MILLENNIUM

JETER

BECKETT PUBLICATIONS, DALLAS, TEXAS

Published by:
Beckett Publications
15850 Dallas Parkway
Dallas, Texas 75248

ISBN: 1-887432-88-4

Beckett® is a registered trademark of
Beckett Publications.

First Edition: March 2000
Beckett Corporate Sales and
Information (972) 991-6657

CONTENTS

FOREWORD

BY NOMAR GARCIAPARRA

As told to Tony Massarotti

People ask me about Derek Jeter all the time, about the fact that we're both shortstops, about the fact that I play for the Red Sox and he plays for the Yankees. I won the American League batting title this year, finishing just one place ahead of Derek, and some people wondered if there was any special meaning for me in beating him. Honestly, I found that question to really be kind of amusing.

After all, I'd rather have his 1999 championship ring.

It's funny the way people build up the competition, like there's a big rivalry among the shortstops, between me and Derek — and Alex Rodriguez, too. I really don't look at it that way. We all get along great and we have so much respect for each other, and each of us just tries to do his own thing. The fact that people saw Derek and me in the batting race this year added to all the talk, I guess, but the batting title wasn't my goal. I think "the

"He's such a great guy, with the way he handles himself," says Garciaparra. "And because of that, he's great for baseball."

rivalry" (if that's what you want to call it) means more to the people outside the game — to the fans and to the media — than it does to the players.

I remember the same kind of stir at the All-Star Game this year, when I was lucky enough to be voted in as the American League starter. It was a nice honor for me, especially because the game was played before my home fans at Fenway Park. Derek finished second in the voting, but, really, either one of us could have started at shortstop. Alex could have started, too, and the same goes for Omar Vizquel of the Cleveland Indians. That whole competition was built up to become a bigger deal than it should have. What does it really matter?

Nomar won the 1999 AL batting title with a .357 average, edging Jeter, who hit .349 for the season.

Derek and Nomar were named to the American League All-Star team in 1999; it was the second trip for both. "At an event like the All-Star Game, we're all there to have fun," says Nomar. "That was a time when we weren't competing with each other, when we were just showing people that we get along."

Nomar would gladly trade in his batting title for one of Derek's championship rings.

Derek has three World Series victories to his credit in his first four full seasons.

Derek and Nomar first met while playing in the Arizona Fall League in 1994. Both had serious credentials — they had been selected in the first round of the draft.

Once the game started, Derek made me laugh. I was in the clubhouse, watching it on TV, when he stepped into the batter's box and started mimicking me at home plate. He tapped his feet back and forth, just like I do, and he couldn't keep a straight face. I thought it was hilarious. It was great. People thought he was making fun of me, but I looked at it as a sign of respect. It was all genuine and good-natured.

At an event like the All-Star Game, we're all there to have fun. That was a time when we weren't competing with each other, when we were just showing people that we get along.

I've known Derek for a while now. We first met in 1994, when we were both playing in

"He's almost always able to put the ball in play," says Garciaparra. "You'll rarely see him hit a pop fly foul for an out; the ball usually goes back in the stands, and that's because he keeps his hands back so well."

Derek was tops in both leagues with 219 hits in 1999. His fifty hits in August made him the first Yankee to accomplish the feat since Joe DiMaggio in July of 1941.

the Arizona Fall League. I had been drafted by the Red Sox earlier that year, and had played only twenty-eight games in the minors before I went to Arizona. Derek had been drafted two years earlier, in 1992. Both of us were shortstops and first-round picks, but anyone who plays in the Arizona Fall League is regarded as a prospect.

I don't really follow other players' careers that closely, but people would talk about Derek, about how quickly he moved up through the Yankees system. And because all of the teams in Arizona are located so closely to one another, you couldn't help but run into some of

"On the basepaths, he's one of the best baserunners you'll find," says Garciaparra. "He's never satisfied with just one base; he's always looking to take the next one."

"If you ask pitchers, they'll tell you he's difficult to pitch to," says Nomar. **"He drives the ball so well to right-center, and he can battle off that inside pitch."**

the guys from other teams in social settings. That's really how you got to know them.

Derek was always good in the field, and he had a good bat, too. That was something I noticed even then. When you see a guy who makes contact most of the time, or has a good eye, that's something you focus on, even if he doesn't drive the ball. Derek definitely drives the ball more now, and it's made a huge difference. I've always thought he had home-run power, and he's definitely become a home-run threat.

Want to hear something funny? In some ways, I blame Derek and Alex for ruining it for guys like me. They hit for average and for power, and it makes it tough for the other guys who play the same position.

People look at those two, and they're setting a new standard. People see that and expect it from everyone. In some ways, it's not fair.

But seriously, Derek's always had that beautiful inside-out swing. He's got a good eye for the ball, and he's a tough out. He keeps his hands in so well. If you ask pitchers, they'll tell you he's difficult to pitch to. He drives the ball so well to right-center, and he can battle off that inside pitch. That's what makes him so effective with two strikes. He's almost always able to put the ball in play. You'll rarely see him hit a pop fly foul for an out; the ball usually goes back in the stands, and that's because he keeps his hands back so well.

Derek's lanky, too. He's definitely got a wiry strength, and he has the speed to steal bases. On the basepaths, he's one of the best baserunners you'll find. He's never satisfied with just one base; he's always looking to take the next one. If you bobble the ball, he'll take an extra base, so you've got to keep your head up.

Know what else? Derek's every bit as good off the field, too. He's such a great guy, with the way he handles himself. And because of that, he's great for baseball. I don't think people want to see just an unbelievable talent anymore. I think they want to see an unbelievable person, and I think Derek gives them that. I think he's a huge draw. I think people come to watch him play, and I think they should.

Certainly, I know I would.

Derek Jeter was named 1996 AL Rookie of the Year and Nomar picked up the award in 1997.

NEW YORK'S FINEST

BY JOE TORRE

As told to Marty Noble

Don Zimmer and I always sit together. We have for four years now. We're on the bench, side by side, almost every day in spring training, the regular season and when we're fortunate enough to be in the postseason. He's been with the Yankees as long as I have. It feels right to have him there.

You get a lot of perks with the job I have, manager of the Yankees. Don Zimmer is one of the perks. He comes with the job, like the uniform. It feels funny when he's not there and comfortable when he is.

Zim is on my left when we're in a first base dugout and on my right when our dugout is on the third base side. People have come to expect us to be there.

It's calming for me to have Zim around. There isn't much that can happen in a game that he hasn't experienced already. I've been in the game a long time. Two thousand will be my forty-first year. But Zim has me beat by eleven years. That's a lot of baseball.

"Zim is on my left when we're in a first base dugout and on my right when our dugout is on the third base side," says Joe Torre. "People have come to expect us to be there."

It's not very often that anyone sits between Zim and me. There's no rule against it. You sit where you want or where you're wanted. But some guys tend to sit in the same places and others fill in around them. Managers and coaches are creatures of habit. They're usually in the same places.

I know I gave Scott Brosius a day off in Anaheim this year, and I told him he could help manage. He sat himself right between us and generally made a pest of himself for nine innings. But the time that always comes to mind was in 1996, our first year with the Yankees and Derek Jeter's first year.

We were in Chicago, it was the eighth inning, and we were down by a run. Derek was on second base with two outs. And he ran. He was caught stealing. They got him when he shouldn't have been running at all. And I was ready to explode. I know I usually look calm, but sometimes you just lose it. I was angry, but I turned to Zim and said, "I'm not going to say anything to the kid tonight. I'll get him tomorrow."

So the inning's over, and he goes to his position without coming into the dugout. Somebody brings his glove to him. So we get through the inning, and he comes off the field.

Does he go hide somewhere? Does he sit down the other end of the dugout? No. He comes right up to us — just comes in, scoots between Zim and me and forces us to make room for him. He's

"He has respect for the game and the people in it," says Joe Torre. "He still calls me "Mr. Torre," and he calls Don "Mr. Zimmer."

there to take his lumps and get it out of the way. I
looked at him, slapped him on the back of his head and
said, "Get outta here."

He knew. He didn't need to be scolded. I was pretty
sure before that we had something special in him. But
what he did that night just reinforced it. I thought that
was extraordinary.

But there's *so much* about Derek Jeter that is special
and different. I've been around a lot of players at various
stages in their careers, but I've never seen one like Derek.
Not at his age. A lot of guys get it eventually; some guys
never get it. But not like him. You knew pretty early on
that he got it. He knew what was right.

He doesn't try to make himself stand out. It just happens naturally because he has such good sense about the
game — how to play it and how to carry himself.

In my first spring training with the Yankees — I
guess it was Derek's second — I didn't know very much
about him except that he had a couple of good years in
the minor leagues and that we had good reports on him
and his makeup.

"He's exceptional in so many ways," says Torre. "The one thing that strikes you — and it struck me — is that older guys look up to him. You don't ever see that."

I hadn't met him. Never seen him play. My big question was about his defense. Could he play the position? He *had* to catch the ball. If he hit .250, fine. But he had to catch it. And I guess his defense had been an issue, the only issue. Otherwise, everyone thought he was ready.

Well, we had Tony Fernandez in camp, too. And when the media asked Derek about the competition for shortstop, he had a great answer. He said, "I have an opportunity to compete for the job."

There was respect in that answer. He didn't think he had anything coming to him because he had been a good player in the minor leagues. He had respect for a veteran player, Tony Fernandez.

That spring, I never thought about his hitting. I just wanted to be comfortable with his defense. And I was. Then on Opening Day, he hits a home run. I said "Wow!" Then he makes a catch on a popup with his back to the infield. I was so impressed by the way he handled everything.

I've never seen players that age handle all of it like he does. No one ever.

He has respect for the game and the people in it. He still calls me "Mr. Torre," and he calls Don "Mr.

Born in Brooklyn, New York, Joe Torre is the first New York City native to manage the Yankees.

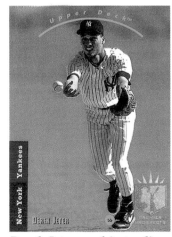

Derek Jeter rookie trading card – 1993 SP #279.

Zimmer." And it's not done with tongue in cheek. He has wonderful parents who have helped make him what he is.

He's exceptional in so many ways. The one thing that strikes you — and it struck me — is that older guys look up to him. You don't ever see that. But there are *so many* things.

"He doesn't try to make himself stand out," says Torre. "It just happens naturally because he has such good sense about the game — how to play it and how to carry himself."

He laughs at himself when he makes a mistake. He makes it all so simple. He makes it easy for others to be around him. And when he makes a mistake, that's it. It doesn't change the way he goes about

Derek played in 1,395.2 innings for the Yankees in 1999, more than any other short-stop in the majors.

"His parents have done a wonderful job, and he sees them as much as he can," says Torre. "You can see he has had very positive influences in his life."

playing. I watched (Dolphins quarterback Dan) Marino throw five interceptions on Thanksgiving. They talked about that a lot. But what I like is that he kept playing his way. A lot of quarterbacks would have shut it down after two interceptions. Marino has confidence. Derek's that way. If something does go against him or bother him, he gets over it pretty quick. He has a buoyancy about him. He puts away the negative as quickly as anyone.

Some of what he is doesn't seem to fit together. He's basically shy. And I know most people don't see him that way. He' so fluid among people. He knows what he is as far as the matinee idol stuff, and he wears it well. He has no pretenses. He's real. He enjoys himself and makes it easy for others to enjoy him.

He seems to understand so much. His parents have

done a wonderful job, and he sees them as much as he can. You can see he has had very positive influences in his life. He became a celebrity very quickly. He was a rookie and six months later he was making plays in the World Series, and in between, it seemed he played a part in every big rally we had.

After that first year, before the offseason, I thought some words of caution might be necessary for a single guy, as popular as he'd become. They weren't . . . I didn't accuse him of anything. I just asked him some questions and suggested he might benefit from my experiences. "Watch out for this and that pothole." He listened. He may have known everything I mentioned, but he listened.

It's all part of handling himself. He has understanding. He hasn't had as much experience at it as some people; he knows what it is to lose. So he never spikes the ball in front of the other team. He'll celebrate but in the right way and among his people. He never does things that say "Look what I did," because he intends to do them again. He doesn't court attention.

But he gets it. He can't help it. Sometimes I marvel at how well he handles it all. We've had a lot of success in the time he's been here, and he's had a lot of success. Sometimes I watch him and I wonder how good he can be and how good it can become for him.

Derek Jeter and Joe Torre have brought three World Series titles to New York in their four years together. That's a record that might even appease team owner George Steinbrenner.

SHOW TIME

BY BUCK SHOWALTER

As told to Mike Tulumello

I first met Derek and his mom and dad in Yankee Stadium when we flew him in. He made a good impression. He said things like "Yes, sir," "No, sir" and "Thank you."

Usually children are going to be a direct reflection of the job their parents have done. And after meeting Mr. and Mrs. Jeter, it was obvious that he was a good kid with a solid foundation and upbringing. And I liked the way he interacted with his siblings. That was impressive about Derek.

Another first impression was that he was a slender guy. A lot of high school guys are pretty slight. A lot of times when you get a guy who's big and strong at eighteen, they've kind of topped out. I spent a lot of time — and I'm sure his mom and dad thought I was nuts — looking at them to see what kind of frame he was going to have as he got older. But that's a standard scouting procedure.

"It didn't take some super scout to see that he had what it took to be an impact player in the big leagues," says Buck Showalter.

Buck Showalter managed the New York Yankees from 1991 through 1995 and was named 1994 American League Manager-of-the-Year by the Baseball Writers Association and *The Sporting News.* In '95 Buck led the Yankees to a wild card berth, the Yankees first post-season appearance since 1981.

A lot of people think scouts go to talk to parents; they go to size them up.

I wanted Derek Jeter and a few other young kids we had, such as Andy Fox and Mariano Rivera and a couple of others, on the roster at the end of the season because I wanted them to be exposed to the wild-card chase.

I was not expecting him to contribute on the field. When you're in that type of crunch time, it's no time to be experimenting with a twenty- or twenty-one-year-old. But I thought it was pretty obvious that Derek was going to get a chance to be a player in the major leagues, and every little thing you can expose him to is a positive. What was impressive was how he was in a soak-it-in mode as opposed to a wild mode. He was very curious and was asking a lot of questions.

I was with all the young guys I had brought up and told them exactly what they were there for and what I

expected them to get out of it. And Derek did. I can remember telling him, "This doesn't happen every year. A lot of teams are just playing out the season. Take this — it's a rare opportunity for you to be exposed to this — soak it in."

I didn't get the chance to manage him much, just that one time, although I spent a lot of time watching him in the Instructional League.

Named the inaugural manager of the expansion Arizona Diamondbacks, Buck Showalter helped lead them to one hundred wins and the NL West pennant in 1999 — in only their second year.

But Derek is a pretty easy guy to manage. You know, when you're looking at players, especially in New York City, you've got to look for things other than just playing ability. They've got to have a strong upbringing, a strong sense of reality and who they are, so they can handle the fickleness of a roller-coaster.

Brian Butterfield, our first-base coach at that time, had been with Derek for quite a while. To this day Derek attributes a lot of his improvement to the instruction he got from Brian. It makes Brian's chest swell up when his instruction is one of the first things Derek brings up. And Brian was there for him when Derek was making fifty to sixty errors in the minor leagues in Greensboro.

Most of the errors were through over-aggressiveness. All good infielders have a clock. They know when to hurry and when to slow down. Derek was adjusting that clock. And whether it was poor fields, or a first baseman who couldn't catch the easy short hops or high throws, there can be a lot of reasons for that happening.

"In Greensboro, he swung the bat real well, but he struggled defensively," says Brian Butterfield, first-base coach of the Yankees when Jeter was pro-moted. "If you look at every shortstop who's playing in the major leagues right now, I think all of them have struggled at one point or another when they were young."

"I just remember what a positive, upbeat kid he was, always smiling, yet working very hard," Brian Butterfield says. "He's one of the finest kids I've ever been around."

There have been a million cases of great shortstops who had high error totals in the minor leagues. Derek just kept working at it, kept listening to instructors. He'd be the first to tell you he's been around some great baseball instructors, people such as Willie Randolph, Clete Boyer and Brian Butterfield. He took it all in.

Sometimes, you get so much information from so many qualified people that it might seem a little contradictory. You don't know what's right and what's wrong. That's where he and Brian hit it off so well. Brian tried to work within his skills, which were, of course, plentiful.

Brian would go up to him and say, "What feels good to you? What did you do wrong here?" He'd let him explain instead of saying, "Hey, you didn't do this or that." He'd say, "OK, you made a great play there. Why was that good? How were you in a position to make that play?" Or, "Why did you throw high there? Did you know that guy didn't run well and you didn't have to hurry?" There are a million things like that.

Derek Jeter and Mariano Rivera were called up to the Yankees from the Triple-A Columbus Clippers at the end of the 1995 season. Buck wanted to give them the experience of a wild-card chase — now they're the cornerstones of the Yankees franchise.

Jeter made an impact at every minor league stop in 1994. The Yankee minor league affiliates combined for a .621 winning percentage with Jeter on the roster and .502 winning percentage without him.

Derek was named *Baseball America*'s minor league player of the year in 1994 after hitting .344 with sixty-eight RBI and fifty stolen bases combined at Triple-A Columbus, Double-A Albany and Class A Tampa.

But instead of saying, "What the heck is wrong with you?" he'd put the onus on him to get better. Instead of saying, "That's the way you've got to do it. It's cut and dried. It's the only way to do it. You can't be successful unless you do it like this." Brian worked within the realm of his skills and made Derek feel responsible for getting better.

A lot of people didn't think Derek would hit for much power, but you never could deny him the chance to do anything. The one thing you want out of a young prospect, as good as he is, you want to have the feeling that he's going to be as good as he's capable of being.

You want to be able to think, 'OK, regardless of what happens, I know this guy will have no outside challenge.' And that includes his approach, his upbringing or his skills.

He was humble, respectful and he didn't think he had all the answers. He knew it was going to be a growing process. Derek tended to blend in. He wasn't popping his gums a lot. He never had a 'look-at-me!' mentality. And through that, his substance was his style. His style wasn't his substance.

I'd look down at the bench during games, and I'd check out the young guys, and he was always looking intently on the field and watching things. I remember he came down one time and said, "That was a hit-and-run right there, and our guy missed the sign, right?" I said, "Yeah." So he had the signs.

His game was still raw. But you could see the skills.

He also was pretty hard on himself. He'd take ground balls and batting practice and if things didn't go just right, he'd get a little frustrated, as most guys do.

Any Tom, Dick or Harry could walk out on the field and see that Derek Jeter could be special. His skills were obvious. It didn't take some super scout to see that he had what it took to be an impact player in the big leagues. You knew this guy is going to be as good as he's capable of being. Just what is that going to be? Only God knows.

Derek Jeter minor league trading card — 1993 Greensboro Hornets Fleer/ProCards #893.

MINOR LEAGUE BATTING STATISTICS

Year	Team	G	AB	H	2B	3B	HR	R	RBI	BB	SO	SB	AVG
1992	Tampa	47	173	35	10	0	3	19	25	19	36	2	.202
	Greensboro	11	37	9	0	0	1	4	4	7	16	0	.243
1993	Greensboro	128	515	152	14	11	5	85	71	58	95	18	.295
1994	Tampa (FSL)	69	292	96	13	8	0	61	39	23	30	28	.329
	Albany	34	122	46	7	2	2	17	13	15	16	12	.377
	Columbus	35	126	44	7	1	3	25	16	20	15	10	.349
1995	Columbus	123	486	154	27	9	2	96	45	61	56	20	.317
Minor League Totals		447	1751	536	78	31	16	307	213	203	264	90	.306

WHOLE NEW BALL GAME

BY CAL RIPKEN JR.

As told to John Delcos

I'm out here in Arizona at a camp. It's a theme vacation and there are current managers here. I spent the first part of the morning teaching these campers about team fundamentals. Buck Showalter and I were out there, and we were talking about Derek Jeter and how he makes this underhand flip. We were demonstrating it to these campers, because shortstops nowadays use this. It's a basic thing, it's a very good weapon, and it's a very good tool.

He makes that play, and gives the ball to the second baseman on the double play as well as anyone, and he does it with ease and grace. It's not a real easy thing to master, and he's done it.

"You never know exactly how far they are going to evolve and how good they are going to be, but I knew he was going to be damn good," says Cal Ripken Jr.

Defensively, I appreciate a lot of his moves and a lot of the things he does. He has the ability to be pretty fundamentally sound and make it look easy. I know how difficult certain plays are and how easy he makes it look.

I think he's more blessed with range and a physical sense than I am. He can move. He has quickness. He's smooth and agile. He's also a good student of the game.

Cal says that Jeter has a "zest to learn" and is always asking questions about pitchers and playing defense.

My first impression of Jeter was that he was raw enough and you could see his talent. You never know exactly how far they are going to evolve and how good they are going to be, but I knew he was going to be damn good.

When I've had conversations with him at All-Star Games, he has a zest to learn. Anybody can ask questions, but he asks pointed questions. That makes me know that he's thinking about the things necessary for positioning, and anticipation, and just basic fundamentals. When he asks me things, he pulls information out of me (in a way) that I know where he's going with it.

A seventeen-time All-Star, Cal Ripken Jr., is baseball's "Iron Man" with a consecutive-games streak of 2,632 to his credit. A two-time AL MVP, he is third among active career hit leaders (2,991), fourth in home runs (402) and second in RBIs (1,571).

How you analyze pitchers and hitters — we've had conversations about that, and that lends itself to positioning. If you know what the tendencies are with a hitter when he has two strikes, what his tendencies are early in the count — you're speaking about facts that are going to help you position yourself. All you have to do is think this way about positioning,

He seems to always be in front of the ball. He almost seems like a magnet to the ball. You have to ask yourself, "Why is that?"

That's the thing they used to say about me, "Cal can make all the routine plays." All of them seem like routine plays, but when you think about it, they all aren't routine plays. By your positioning and your anticipation, and the style in which you catch it, you make those plays seem routine.

"He has the ability to be pretty fundamentally sound and make it look easy," Ripken Jr. says. "I know how difficult certain plays are and how easy he makes it look."

In 1990 Cal had the highest single-season fielding percentage (.996) by a shortstop in Major League history, with only three errors in 680 total chances. After playing fifteen years at shortstop, Cal moved to third base in 1996, Derek's first full season in the majors.

Offensively, you never know, but he possesses a lot of power. You don't always know where it is, but he has opposite field power, he has center field power.

That part of his game could develop and he could be a real great home run hitter. But as far as being a total player, he's a high-impact player. He's one of those guys you want to grab and build your team around.

I think he's a very mature kid. He must have had some very good teachers, not only in the aspect of baseball, but in life issues and dealing with off-the-field baseball stuff. He seems to handle things well. That's a tool and advantage that he really needs in New York. From

"It says a lot about his character that he cares about the game ... about his willingness to work," says Ripken Jr. "He has a love and a passion and respect for the game."

the outside, you would think that he's older than he really is by the way he handles himself.

I think it's a healthy competition he has with Seattle's Alex Rodriguez and Boston's Nomar Garciaparra. They are all great players. They bring a lot of excitement to the position of shortstop, but they also have a lot of importance to their teams. They are in the middle of their lineup offensively, and they are a critical component of their success defensively. They represent the position at a new level unbelievably well. They are actually redefining it.

I remember, I used to watch my contemporaries, Detroit's Alan Trammell and Milwaukee's Robin Yount, and try to pick from their game and add to my game. You're always in a little quiet competition for your position, and I know that exists with Derek and A-Rod. I'm not so certain it exists with Nomar, but I have to believe it's there. It's a quiet motivator.

Always at the top of "Most Popular Player" lists, Cal Ripken Jr. is often willing to sign autographs for fans. When it comes to autographs, Jeter has also been accessible at the ballpark.

Derek has a career stolen base success rate of seventy-two percent with his best year coming in 1998. That year he stole thirty bases and was caught just six times for a success rate of eighty-six percent.

Jeter is a throwback player who's willing to do anything for the good of the team — including bunt when he's asked to.

1998 Starting Lineup 12-inch Derek Jeter sports action figure.

They like each other and I know they watch and pick from each other's games, because they are only slightly different. They are similar in that they are unbelievable offensive players and they are unbelievable defensive players, but they all do things slightly different. That's good. That's a healthy competition and it makes for growth in everyone's games.

Jeter has said he wants to leave the game better than he found it. That's admirable. It's not short term. It's not quick fix. It says a lot about his character that he cares about the game ... about his willingness to work. He has a love and a passion and respect for the game. With him being a proud player and a perfectionist of sorts, he wants to be as good as he can be and leave that mark with the game.

If I were to give him one piece of advice, it would be to keep the spirit of the game. You have to have a love of the game.

I'm not saying that in the literal sense. I'm saying that in how it makes you feel, how it drives you ... that spirit and joy that you feel, that passion and love of the sport. Always keep feeding that, because that's what drives you, what pushes you. Don't forget that the game is fun ... that's part of the spirit. The game is meant to be fun. Never lose the passion, never lose the understanding that it is fun. That's what's going to carry you.

"As far as being a total player, he's a high-impact player," Ripken Jr. says. "He's one of those guys you want to grab and build your team around."

PRODIGY IN PINSTRIPES

BY PHIL RIZZUTO

As told to Dan Schlossberg

Derek Jeter definitely has a Yankee pinstripe inside of him. He wants to be a Yankee his whole career. Every year he's gotten better and better, hit for a higher average and increased his home run production. And he's well liked not only by the Yankees players but all the other players who play against him.

The press loves him. And you know how the kids love him — the girls just go crazy.

He's the perfect man for the Yankees, the logical guy to be the No. 1 man.

For years, the Yankees have always had one man stand out. Way back, it was Babe Ruth. Then Lou Gehrig, followed by Joe DiMaggio. After that it was

With eleven World Series wins between them, Phil Rizzuto and Derek Jeter have been field generals for some of the Yankees' greatest teams of all time.

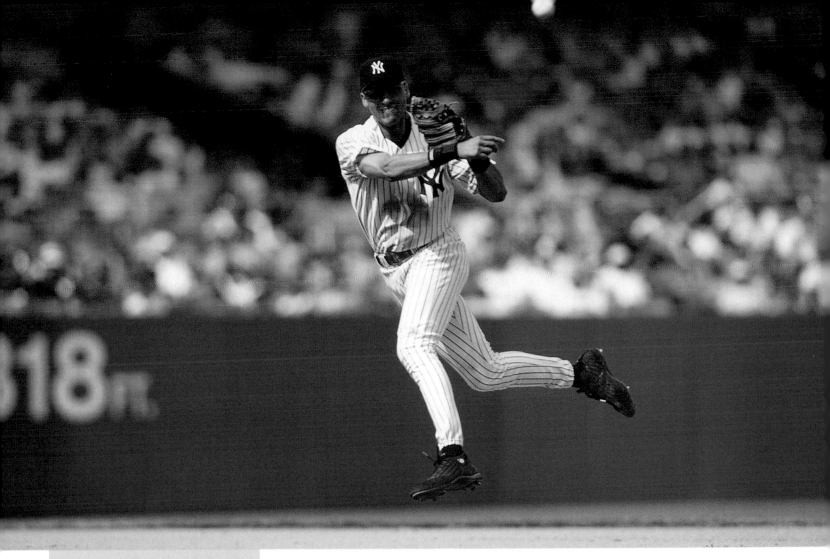

Mickey Mantle. Yogi (Berra) had several big years, and Roger Maris. There was always somebody, far and above superior to the rest of the team.

And Jeter is the one right now. The sky's the limit for him: I see batting titles, All-Star Games, World Series appearances, and MVP awards in his future.

I know the Yankees have a young kid named (Alfonso) Soriano who is supposed to be a sensational shortstop. But I don't see how the Yankees could even consider moving Derek Jeter to another position. I think it would break the kid's heart if he had to play third base. But I also think he would do it if the Yankees asked him. That's how much of a team man he is. I can't see that happening.

Elected to the Baseball Hall of Fame in 1994, "scooter" was a five-time all-star and helped the Yankees to ten American League Pennants. Since retiring, Rizzuto has spent more than forty years as a Yankee broadcaster.

Jeter's like Yogi. Yogi didn't seem to care about anything. He was loose and relaxed when he played and enjoyed the game. The same is true of Jeter; you can see how much he enjoys it. He's the first one to pop out of the dugout to congratulate someone who's hit a home run, he does so many little things like that.

I knew Derek Jeter was going to be a great ballplayer the first year he came up from the minors to finish a season with the Yankees (fifteen games at the end of the 1995 campaign).

I got into a bit of trouble because I said something about him to Buck Showalter, who was managing the club at the time. When the team got into the playoffs and had a chance to get into the World Series, I said, "Why don't you play [Darryl] Strawberry — who was also up at that time — and Jeter? Jeter can't hurt you."

I forget who they had playing shortstop at that time — oh yes, Tony Fernandez. He wasn't too bad. But Showalter as much as said, "Keep your big mouth shut." He didn't quite say it that way but I knew he didn't want to go into it. He said the kid didn't have enough experience. That broke my heart.

"For years, the Yankees have always had one man stand out," Rizzuto says. "Way back, it was Babe Ruth. Then Lou Gehrig, followed by Joe DiMaggio. After that it was Mickey Mantle. Yogi (Berra) had several big years, and Roger Maris."

I study shortstops: That's all I studied when I used to broadcast the games. I followed every shortstop. Naturally, day after day, watching the same team in the same place, you could tell things about Derek Jeter. He just improved steadily every year, and, like Don Mattingly, made himself great. He's always working to be a better ballplayer.

The thing that gets me is his height (6'3") and how he's able to commit on those slow rollers. For a man that tall to get down and make a good throw isn't easy. He's got those long arms, he dives, and he takes line-drive base hits away.

I've never seen anybody throw a guy out like he does, going into the hole, deep on the outfield grass, jumping up in the air like a football quarterback, firing, and getting fast runners at first base.

"He's the first one to pop out of the dugout to congratulate someone who's hit a home run, he does so many little things like that," says Rizzuto.

He does everything; he's especially good on double plays.

Even in my best years, I couldn't carry Jeter's glove. Number one, I'm only 5'6". I couldn't get those high line drives. A ball hit deep at shortstop, I'd have to throw to third base where we'd get a lot of those slow sluggers like Baltimore had. Or I'd toss to Billy Johnson or Bobby Brown and they'd throw the guy out.

Jeter doesn't need to do any of that stuff. I didn't have the arm Jeter has. I had to get rid of the ball in a hurry.

I know there are three great shortstops in the American League with Jeter, Nomar Garciaparra, and Alex Rodriguez. Naturally, I pick Jeter as the best, the real All-Star, because I see him every day.

When it comes to picking the best shortstop in the league, Rizzuto goes with Jeter — the one he sees play nearly every day.

"He just improved steadily every year, and, like Don Mattingly, made himself great," says Rizzuto. "He's always working to be a better ballplayer."

Parades and victory speeches are becoming a regular occurrence for Derek. He's helped the Yankees to three World Series victories in his four full years in the majors.

I was lucky: I was in ten World Series in the thirteen years I played. Jeter's in almost the same situation. The team has made the postseason in all four of his full seasons.

Getting to the World Series is such a great feeling. You can't beat it. It's the greatest thing in the world for a ballplayer to be able to play every year and get into a World Series almost every year.

When we had all those World Series with the Brooklyn Dodgers (in the 1940s and 1950s), we not only expected to win the pennant but also the Series. When we finally lost one in 1955, we didn't know what to do or how to act. The Yankees weren't used to losing.

Today, with cable television, the Internet, and modern communications technology, there's much more

"I want to thank the Good Lord for making me a Yankee"
—Joe DiMaggio

"Derek Jeter definitely has a Yankee pin-stripe inside of him," Rizzuto says. "He wants to be a Yankee his whole career."

exposure than I had. When you're in the World Series, you know you're going to be seen all over the world. You try harder and you just hope you play well.

Derek Jeter has done that and should do it many more times in the future.

Derek Jeter Salvino's Bammer plush collectible.

MANHATTAN TRANSFER

BY CHUCK KNOBLAUCH

As told to John Delcos

When you've played against somebody for awhile and then he becomes a teammate, it's only natural that your perception of him would change, because you spend more time with him and you're able to get to know him better.

When you play against somebody who's a rookie, you don't know the things he's capable of doing. My perception of Derek has definitely changed from when I first saw him as a rookie four years ago to when I was traded here two years ago. It has changed not only because I've become his teammate, but also because he's become a better player.

You really don't get to know another player — either on the field or off the field — until you get to play with him every day. It's hard to judge a young player when he's on another team. It's a bad way to judge anybody, because you're only seeing him, in reality, eleven or twelve times a year. Guys play well against certain teams

"The great players tend to do that — they raise the level of the guys around them," says Chuck Knoblauch.

Chuck Knoblauch was the 1991 American League Rookie of the Year — Derek earned that same award in 1996.

and guys don't. If you catch a guy not playing well, you might not think he's pretty good. It's a little different if the player is a veteran, because you would have seen him over the course of a few years.

I think getting to know Derek off the field has helped our relationship on the field. We're on the same page more and have a better idea of what is going on out there. We're comfortable with each other and support each other.

For a double-play combination, getting familiar with each other is always a work in progress. If you ask

the greatest double-play combinations, they would say
they are always continuing to get better as the years go
by. It really didn't take a whole lot of time for Derek and
I to become comfortable with each other. We're both
pretty easy to work with and not too picky where we
need the ball on a double play. It's just communication.
We're constantly talking about situations during the
game and between pitches.

When Derek first came up, you could definitely tell
he had ability by the things he would do. He's definitely
become a better player since then.

What makes him the player he is? The first thing is
talent. You have to have talent. But I think the way he
goes about things, his work ethic and his desire to be the
best he can be, will enable him to continue to get better.

"Chuck is one of the best second basemen of all time, defensively," Jeter says. "I played with ten second basemen in my first two years, so it gives me a good opportunity to play with one guy and get familiar with him."

No matter what sport you're playing, if you're playing around great players, they definitely are going to make the people around them better. The great players tend to do that — they raise the level of the guys around them.

In baseball, it might not be noticed as much as basketball where you're out on the floor with four other guys. But, it's there in more subtle ways. Throughout the course of the season you might see some things — mostly in the lineup. [Knoblauch being a base stealer, he's helped when Jeter protects him by fouling off a pitch when he gets a poor jump and by hitting behind the runner and keeping

"If I had to pick a premier double-play combination [in today's game]," says thirteen-time Gold Glover Ozzie Smith, "it would probably be Knoblauch and Jeter because of their experience. They're the best Yankee combo in a long time."

With Knoblauch on base, Jeter will help protect him by fouling off a pitch when he gets a poor jump.

the ball on the ground.] And, even defensively, if you're playing next to a great player — he might be able to get to a ball so that you don't have to.

For a player to have the respect of other players means a great deal, and Derek has the respect of everybody here. If you have the respect of your peers, and especially your teammates, it takes the relationship, or the level of play, up a notch. If

Derek helped turn eighty-eight double plays in 1999 and has had more than eighty in each of his four full seasons for the Yankees.

you know you can count on the guy next to you, then things are obviously going to be better than the reverse situation.

We have a great deal of respect for Derek. He goes about the game the right way. He works at it. He plays hard and he knows the game.

Does Derek have the potential to be a superstar?

1997 Donruss Signature Series Century Marks autograph trading card.

Yeah, I would assume so. Define a star first. Is he head and shoulders above everybody else? Would a superstar then be head and shoulders above all the stars? With a superstar, there's a charisma outside the obvious talent that makes people want to follow and gravitate toward the guy. He's a guy who can take over a game and control it just by his mere presence. He can take over and dominate a game in one way or another.

Derek certainly has that capability, whether it's defensively or with his bat.

"For a player to have the respect of other players means a great deal, and Derek has the respect of everybody here," says Chuck.

A GLOVE STORY

BY OZZIE SMITH

As told to John Delcos

What kind of shortstop is Derek Jeter? Well, a very effective one, to be sure. I think he's a sleeker and leaner model of a Cal Ripken. He's out of the Cal Ripken mold in that he's tall and rangy, has a great arm, covers a lot of ground and he's a great offensive player.

I think the guys that are playing today are much better offensive players than the shortstops were when I first came up. The position has evolved to that. For a long time it was noted as just a defensive position, so generally the best defensive players — or the guys with the best hands — were usually put in the middle of the infield.

God has blessed him with both a great pair of hands and the ability to hit, too. He's got power. He can hit for average. It's one of those blessed things that have happened to three or four guys who happen to be in the big leagues at the same time and playing the same position.

Jeter found his power stroke in 1999, hitting twenty-four home runs and thirty-seven doubles. That's coming from a minor league career in which he hit sixteen home runs — over four seasons.

Derek, and Nomar (Garciappara) and Alex (Rodriguez) are all incredibly gifted players.

People have asked me, "If you're going to start a team, which one would you start with?" I always tell them you couldn't go wrong with any of those guys because of their abilities to present you with not only great defense, but great offense as well. These are guys who can hit the ball out of the ballpark ... and play good defense ... and play well enough for you to win.

While there is a premium placed on offensive players, defense is defense. You still need defense. We've always known the importance of it. I think I had a small part of reinforcing the importance of it. Most people look at momentum as being simply offensive. However, I think

people have come to know — especially people who had a chance to see me play — that momentum can be turned on

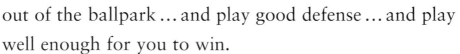

Ozzie Smith is arguably the greatest defensive shortstop of all time. He was a fifteen-time NL all-star and won thirteen consecutive gold gloves at shortstop. Yet he was almost as well known for his trademark flip as he ran on the field.

defensive plays, too. That's one of the things I prided myself on — I was able to change the momentum of a game. This is the thing that these guys can do.

From what I've been able to see from watching him the last three or four years is that he's doing everything well. He's able to go into the hole and make the strong

throw, he's able to charge the ball and make a play with the bare hand and he's able to turn the double play.

The one thing that every shortstop should be able to do well is go to his left better than he goes to his right. What you need to do is work on going to your right and become as good going that way — away from the play — as you are going to it. Derek has become very astute at that.

You know you've made it big when you have a cereal named after you. In 1999 Famous Fixins introduced "Jeter's," a frosted flakes cereal. A portion of cereal's proceeds are donated to Jeter's Turn 2 Foundation.

He's also very good at charging the ball and getting rid of the ball. He's doing all the things he needs to do to be a good consistent shortstop at the big league level.

One of the most impressive things about him is his ability to handle the pressure at this level, especially playing in New York. How he's done that speaks for itself. Whenever I've had a chance to sit and chat with him … you can tell he keeps everything in perspective. I think it's a reflection of the way he plays, too. It's not getting too high, and not getting too low and being consistent. And, being consistent doesn't necessarily mean just being consistent on the field, but being consistent off the field as well.

We look at it as that's a hard thing to do for somebody who's so young, but some people are older than others of the same age. Some young guys don't understand it, but he's just the opposite. He's played

"It's one of those blessed things that have happened to three or four guys who happen to be in the big leagues at the same time and playing the same position," Ozzie says. "Derek, and Nomar (Garciappara) and Alex (Rodriguez) are all incredibly gifted players."

"**Momentum can be turned on defensive plays, too,**" says Smith. "**That's one of the things I prided myself on — I was able to change the momentum of a game. This is the thing that these guys can do.**"

much more than his years. He's conducted himself much more than his years. And that probably has a lot to do with his upbringing.

He's doing what he's supposed to be doing. He's going out there and playing sound, consistent baseball every day in a town where it has been hard for a lot of other guys. I think, because of his maturity, and his ability, and his mindset, that he's been able to do it ... and do it very, very well.

"He's able to go into the hole and make the strong throw, he's able to charge the ball and make a play with the bare hand and he's able to turn the double play," Ozzie says.

Derek is at his best when playing in a hostile environment. He led the major leagues with a .369 batting average on the road.

"One of the most impressive things about him is his ability to handle the pressure at this level, especially playing in New York," says Smith. "How he's done that speaks for itself."

It's hard when you have that much attention paid to you that you don't let it get to you. The most important thing is to avoid doing more than you're capable of. Just be yourself. And I think, he's just being himself. What you see is a direct reflection of how he feels, and how he goes about his work each and every day … goes about his life each and every day. It's a great feeling to have people respect you for who, and what, you are, and what you bring.

CAREER FIELDING STATISTICS

Year	Team	Games	Games Started	Total Chances	Put Outs	Assists	Errors	Double Plays	Fielding Percentage
1995	NYY	15	14	53	17	34	2	7	.962
1996	NYY	157	156	710	244	444	22	83	.969
1997	NYY	159	159	719	244	457	18	87	.975
1998	NYY	148	148	625	223	393	9	82	.986
1999	NYY	158	158	635	230	391	14	88	.978
Totals		637	635	2,742	958	1,719	65	347	.976

While there is pressure in playing in New York, I think being on this team in particular has helped him. In any high-profile situation, it's nice not to be the only guy that the focus is on … you try to spread that around.

When you talk about a team, you look at this Yankee team starting in 1996, and that's exactly what it's been. It's been a team. They don't have a lot of superstars, but they have a lot of guys who know what their jobs are and know how to go about getting their job done each day. This organization has really surrounded itself with quality people, and Derek is one of them.

Derek has said that when he retires he wants to leave the game better than when he came in. That's really the goal. As a player, I think that if you work on being as consistent as you possibly can … if you play the game hard every day … if you give it your all every day, that the best you can hope for is that you can be considered for the Hall of Fame.

STAR POWER

BY ROGER CLEMENS

As told to John Delcos

I think I can assess people pretty good, and I can see the fondness that everybody has — especially his teammates — toward Derek. You see, there's a joy in his game. He's a player who doesn't seem scared to succeed, and he really wants to find how high he can take his game.

At the point he is now, which is at an extremely high level, he seems to enjoy it up there and likes where he's at. That just tells you the guy is going to continue to push harder and reach higher to maximize his potential. There are some other guys who will never find that because they don't have that drive.

Not being afraid to succeed is one attribute that's the difference between a star and a superstar. Some guys are just content where they are at in their careers. I just don't think Derek's ever going to be content. He knows he can get stronger, even with the kind of years that he's had, he knows he can get better. He's fun to watch. You

want a guy like that on your team — a guy who comes to play every day.

I think that as each year goes by, his life is going to change in many ways. It will change not only on the field, but probably away from the field as well. It'll be fun, as a teammate, to watch how that goes. I remember in my first three or four years, Dwight Evans and Jimmy Rice were at the stage I am now. They told me what I might expect in this game. They told me what it means to play at this level and how important it is to enjoy this game and to have fun at it. They were guys I respected.

You earn your respect from your peers. It's not something that is not just given ... you have to go out and earn it. I think it's how you treat people. I think you should treat people with respect. I was brought up that way and I'm sure Derek was brought up that way too.

Roger Clemens has won the American League Cy Young award a record five times (1986, '87, '91, '97 and '98) and the AL MVP award once (1986).

While some short-stops need to plant their feet to make a play to first, at six-foot-three Derek has the strength to grab a ball in the hole and fire it to first while jumping.

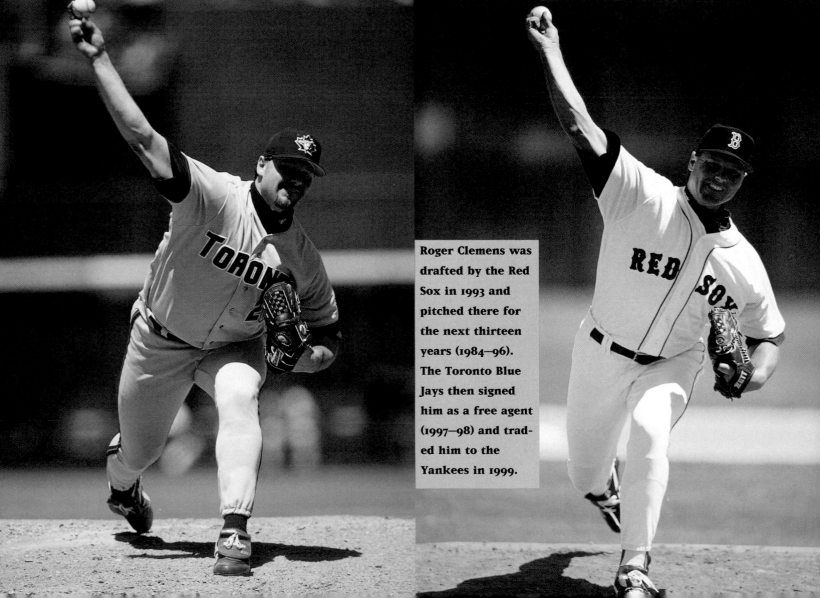

Roger Clemens was drafted by the Red Sox in 1993 and pitched there for the next thirteen years (1984–96). The Toronto Blue Jays then signed him as a free agent (1997–98) and traded him to the Yankees in 1999.

"Derek isn't small, but he's not Mark McGwire," Roger says. "He puts every bit of strength into it. He has strong hands. He's just gifted and he's put it together."

"When I first came into camp, the first two guys who were busting my chops were Knobby [Chuck Knoblauch] and Jeter," says Clemens.

You pick your spots when to have fun and when to be kids in a kids' game. When I first came into camp, the first two guys who were busting my chops were Knobby (Chuck Knoblauch) and Jeter. They were getting after me, wearing the catcher's gear when they first hit off me in the batting cage. That was fun, and that made me feel welcome. They made me feel a part of things.

But, there's a time to have fun and there's a time to work and know your business. You have to be able to juggle that. Derek is a young man who has been able to do that.

There are a lot of things thrown at you when you're young and it's your first time in this league and you're try-ing to make a name for yourself, but he's been able

Jeter has graced the covers of some of the nation's top magazines. That trend doesn't look to end anytime soon.

With Jeter's strong defense behind him, Clemens has one less thing to worry about when facing a batter. From 1996–98 Jeter's errors decreased while his fielding percentage increased.

When "The Rocket" joined Jeter, Joe Torre and the rest of the Yankees, he did it with the hope of winning something he didn't have — a World Series ring. He had his chance quickly and made the most of it, winning the deciding game of the 1999 World Series.

to handle it. And, I think it's probably because of his upbringing. I think it has to do with the fact that he has a lot of character. The bottom line is he has a big heart.

There are a lot of responsibilities that go with playing in the majors, and he's been able to juggle those and still do his work on the field. If all that other stuff got in the way of his livelihood — which is this game right now — then it would probably upset him a little bit. But, he's been able to handle a lot of distractions that come his way, and because of that, he's been able to develop into a great ballplayer. And, he's going to get even better.

Right now you're seeing his potential. You look at his frame and wonder where he gets his power. He hit some balls this year for home runs, and opposite-field homers, that are hard to believe. I heard about the ball he hit in the upper deck here (in 1998, he hit an opposite field home run in the upper deck at Yankee Stadium, something Mickey Mantle didn't even do).

Derek isn't small, but he's not Mark McGwire. He puts every bit of strength into it. He has strong hands. He's just gifted and he's put it together. I'm glad I'm here to see it.

THE FUTURE IS NOW

BY BOB COSTAS

As told to John Delcos

As great as the Yankees are as a team, the only player on their team — with the exception of Roger Clemens, whose Hall of Fame credentials were established elsewhere — who I confidently predict will be a Hall of Famer is Derek Jeter.

With a shortstop with numbers like Jeter's, barring injury and if he keeps doing what he's established so far, he can't miss.

Obviously, Mariano Rivera could be, and Bernie Williams, I guess, could be, but Jeter is the only Yankee clearly stamped a Hall of Famer. A player who you could see someday out there in Monument Park with Ruth and Gehrig and DiMaggio and Mantle.

You have to recognize the differences in the eras when comparing Jeter and Mantle. Baseball had a different kind of romance, and a different kind of mystique in the 1950s and '60s than it does now, and Mantle was a home run hitter of mythic proportions.

But, Jeter has the Hall of Fame ability, and a nearly unique combination of qualities in that he has a certain hipness. He's a handsome guy…he's a stylish guy…he's a Man About Town in New York. But, there are certain classic qualities about him, too. He's not a brash, in-your-face prototypical late '90s athlete. He's humble and soft-spoken. He shows an appreciation for history and for his predecessors.

He has a bit of the DiMaggio grace and reserve about him. There is something about his presence and

personality where you could see him fit in 1959 as well as 1999.

I think those qualities would be evident in a less glamorous media market, but fewer people would pay attention and the setting would be far less classic.

Setting is important. Run the one hundred in nine-flat at a track meet is one thing, but do it at the Olympics and it gives an entirely different aura to what you have done. The same thing is true with Derek. He's in the Pinstripes, in Yankee Stadium, figuratively in the shadow of the Monuments. And, he comes into the public spotlight at a time when his team is clearly the best team in baseball and clearly one of the best baseball teams ever.

Bob Costas, with NBC since 1980, is considered a premier baseball broadcaster and analyst. He has covered the NFL, the NBA and college basketball as well as Major League Baseball. Costas has hosted just about every major sporting event, including numerous World Series, Super Bowls, NBA Championships and Olympics.

"He's hip and traditional simultaneously, and that's something that is very difficult to accomplish," Costas says.

"It's interesting, in that this is the hardest Yankee team to dislike, maybe ever and certainly of this generation," says Costas.

Derek's a fan attraction both at Yankee Stadium and on the road. He draws autograph hounds and groupies like a rock star.

Here's a guy who's had four full years in the major leagues and his team wins the World Series three times.

I think, as the product of interracial parents, he has tremendous crossover appeal ... cross-cultural appeal ... transracial appeal. He is cool and classic at the same time. I don't think you can make yourself be that. I don't think you can decide to be that and work toward being that. It's just kind of the way he is. He's hip and traditional simultaneously, and that's something that is very difficult to accomplish.

It's interesting, in that this is the hardest Yankee team to dislike, maybe ever and certainly of this generation, because Joe Torre's image became the prevailing image of the team. Then you look around at the team itself, and — no jerks.

Built in 1923, Yankee Stadium, "the house that Ruth built," is one of the oldest and most easily recognized sporting venues in the world.

Even someone who has been in trouble like Darryl Strawberry, when he returns he always acts polite and humble. Many people loved Reggie Jackson and other people couldn't stand him — brash. Thurman Munson, hard-nosed guy — some people loved him and he rubbed other people the wrong way. Billy Martin was the same deal. And, George Steinbrenner was obviously unpopular in many quarters.

But now, the prevailing image of the team is, 'Who doesn't like Joe Torre?' Or Don Zimmer? Or Bernie Williams? Or Tino Martinez? Or Jeter? These guys are as benign as people can be.

CAREER BATTING STATISTICS

Year	G	AB	H	2B	3B	HR	TB	R	RBI	BB	SO	OBP	SLG	AVG
1995	15	48	12	4	1	0	18	5	7	3	11	.294	.375	.250
1996	157	582	183	25	6	10	250	104	78	48	102	.370	.430	.314
1997	159	654	190	31	7	10	265	116	70	74	125	.370	.405	.291
1998	149	626	203	25	8	19	301	127	84	57	119	.384	.481	.324
1999	158	627	219	37	9	24	346	134	102	91	116	.438	.552	.349
Totals	638	2537	807	122	31	63	1180	486	341	273	473	.389	.465	.318

Costas says that Jeter has a "bit of the DiMaggio grace and reserve about him." He also may have some of the DiMaggio bat. In 1998 Jeter became only the second Yankee to score more than one hundred runs in each of his first two seasons. The other — Joe DiMaggio in 1936—37.

"He's in the Pinstripes, in Yankee Stadium, figuratively in the shadow of the Monuments," says Costas about Jeter.

Whether it's watching the New York Knicks play at the Garden with Billy Crystal and Alec Baldwin or meeting President Clinton at the White House after winning the World Series, Derek is always in the spotlight.

You can find Jeter's mug in nearly any conceivable place, including on this peanut butter jar.

Jeter has said when he retires he wants to leave Major League Baseball in better shape than when he entered the game and he wants to leave as a positive force. That's a very encouraging thing. I don't know that any one person, or very few anyway — Michael Jordan changed the direction of the NBA, and Babe Ruth and Jackie Robinson changed baseball — are capable of doing that. But, each in his own way, and Jeter's way would be larger than most because he has the talent, and the team and the stage to have a positive impact. He can definitely be one of the players people point to when they list the things that are right about baseball.

Playing in the largest sports media market for the world's most widely recognized team, Jeter is constantly under a microscope. Photo shoots, commercial tapings and media interviews come with the territory.

EDITORIAL CREDITS

John Delcos, who interviewed Cal Ripken Jr., Chuck Knoblauch, Ozzie Smith, Roger Clemens and Bob Costas, covers the New York Yankees and Major League Baseball for the *Gannett Journal News* in Westchester, NY.

Marty Noble, who interviewed Joe Torre, is a reporter for *Newsday* and has covered baseball in New York since 1974. He had the opportunity to report on Joe Torre during his tenure as manager of the New York Mets.

Tony Massarotti, who interviewed Nomar Garciaparra, is a reporter at *The Boston Herald* and has been covering the Red Sox since the start of the 1995 season.

Dan Schlossberg, who interviewed Phil Rizzuto, is baseball editor of *The Encyclopedia Americana* and author of twenty-one books, including *The New Baseball Catalog*.

Mike Tulumello, who interviewed Buck Showalter, is a sports writer for the *East Valley Tribune* in Arizona. He is the author of two books, *Breaking the Rules* (1996) about Charles Barkley and the Phoenix Suns and *The Sports Fan's Guide to America* (1999), a guidebook giving fans tips on tickets, transportation, sports bars and nightlife.

PHOTOGRAPHY

Al Tielemans/*Sports Illustrated*: 68
Allen Kee/BRSP: 9, 42, 43, 74, 76 (bottom)
AP/Wide World Photos: 12 (bottom), 14 (top), 35, 49, 79, 96 (top), 112, 127 (top)
Baseball Hall of Fame: 72 (top left), 72 (top right), 72 (bottom)
Bob Rosato: 10, 39 (bottom), 71, 73, 84, 109 (top), 109 (bottom)
Bob Rosato/Major League Baseball: 41 (bottom), 77, 83
Chuck Solomon/*Sports Illustrated*: 63
David Seeling/Allsport: 21, 82
David Durochik: 62 (top)
Duomo: 62 (bottom), 65, 78
E.J. Camp/Corbis/Outline: 2
Icon Sports Media: 114
James Lathrop: 38
James Schnepf/Liaison Agency: 120
Jed Jacobsohn/Allsport: 125 (bottom)
Jim McLean: 37, 44 (top), 44 (bottom), 45, 46, 47, 48
John Biever/*Sports Illustrated*: 85 (bottom)
John Klein/SportsChrome: 100
John Williamson/Major League Baseball: 18, 53, 56, 86 (top)
Michael Ponzini: 14 (bottom)
NBLA/Major League Baseball: 75 (left)
NY Daily News: 24, 32, 41, 46 (bottom), 70 (top), 108, 118, 126
Profile/Major League Baseball: 70 (bottom)

Rich Pilling/Major League Baseball: 12 (top), 69, 76 (top), 86 (bottom), 93 (bottom)
Rob Tringali Jr./SportsChrome: 11 (top), 19, 27, 29, 58 (top), 58 (bottom), 82 (bottom), 85 (top), 87 (top), 94, 123
Ron Vesely Photography: 13 (bottom), 16, 17, 55, 63 (top), 67, 97, 105, 122 (bottom)
Ron Vesely/Ron Vesely Photography: 31, 64, 81, 93 (top), 95 (bottom), 115
SportsChrome: 4–5, 59 (left), 96 (bottom)
Sports Imagery: 60, 102, 106–107, 113, 121
Steve Crandall: 28 (bottom), 33, 75 (right), 98–99, 110 (top)
Tom DiPace: 6, 11 (bottom), 13, 15, 23, 25, 26, 30, 34, 39 (top), 40, 50, 54, 57, 59 (right), 61, 87 (bottom), 88 (left), 88 (right), 89, 91, 92, 95 (top), 103, 110 (bottom left), 110 (bottom right), 111, 117, 119, 124, 125 (top)
Vincent Laforet/Allsport: 101
V.J. Lovero/*Sports Illustrated*: 28 (top)
Walter Iooss Jr./*Sports Illustrated*: cover, 1, 122 (top)
William Garrow/Sports Imagery: 127 (bottom)

Doug Kale provided Derek Jeter memorabilia for this book.